Where Animals Live

The World of Honeybees

Words by Virginia Harrison

Adapted from Christopher O'Toole's
The Honeybee in the Meadow

Photographs by
Oxford Scientific Films

Gareth Stevens Publishing
Milwaukee

Contents

Note: The use of a capital letter for a bee's name indicates that it is a *species* of bee (for example, Western Honeybee). The use of a lower-case, or small, letter means that it is a member of a larger *group* of bees.

Meadow Bees

If you are ever in a meadow on a lazy, hot summer's day, you will hear the busy hum of the many insects that visit its flowers. Bumblebees and honeybees buzz around collecting flower pollen and nectar. Honeybees turn the nectar into honey.

This meadow in the Colorado Rocky Mountains is just one example of bee habitats around the world. There are at least 20,000 different species, or kinds of bees, and five of these are honeybee species. Western Honeybees were brought to North America with the European settlers of the 1620s. Today they are kept by beekeepers in many parts of the world.

3

Bees and Flowers

Bees depend on the pollen and nectar of flowers for their food, and most flowers depend on bees for fertilization. As bees travel in search of food, they pick up the pollen from one flower in their tiny body hairs. They then brush it off on another flower. This process, called pollination, is needed before seeds can grow.

It is the job of the worker honeybees — always female — to collect nectar and pollen. They are attracted to the brightly colored, pleasant-smelling flowers of the meadow. Dark lines on some flower petals, called nectar guides, point to the nectar.

When a worker collects pollen, she brushes it from the hairs on her *thorax* and deposits it in baskets on her hind legs (above and below). She must visit many flowers to fill both baskets.

In addition to nectar and pollen, bees collect a sticky substance called propolis. Propolis is produced by certain buds and plant wounds. Bees use it like glue to help build their nests and to fill up cracks in the hive.

Usually, the bee will visit the same kind of flower on each trip. This increases the chances of pollination for that flower species.

The Honeybee's Body

The honeybee is a social insect, with colonies of family groups. Each colony consists of an egg-laying female, called a *queen* (above), many thousands of workers, and for a short period, males, or *drones*. These three groups, called *castes*, each have special tasks. Their bodies differ slightly, depending on their task. The worker bee (below) has a long tongue, called a *proboscis*, used in probing for nectar.

The head carries two large *compound eyes*.
Each *eye* is made of many facets, each with its
own lens. This kind of *eye* is particularly good
at seeing movement. Workers and drones need
very good eyesight. That is why their eyes have
many more thousands of facets than the queen,
who spends most of her time in the nest.

On top of each honeybee's head are three
simple eyes, called *ocelli*, which sense changes
in light. Between the compound eyes are
antennae. They are used for feeling and for
smelling *pheromones*, with which honeybees
communicate. The antennae are made of
twelve to thirteen *segments* each.

In the middle of the honeybee's body is the thorax, which has two wings, three pairs of legs, and the muscles that move these parts.

The bee's wings can beat about 200 times per second. You can see the dark veins, which make the wing rigid so the bee can fly.

The abdomen, which is at the rear of the honeybee, is divided into segments. The abdomen contains the honey stomach and the gut, and, in the drone, the male sex organs. Queens' and workers' abdomens hold the *ovaries*, where eggs are produced.

The stinger, which is on the tip of every honeybee's abdomen, has a poison gland and very sharp barbs. In the picture below, the bee has stung a person's finger and has left the sting behind to continue pumping venom.

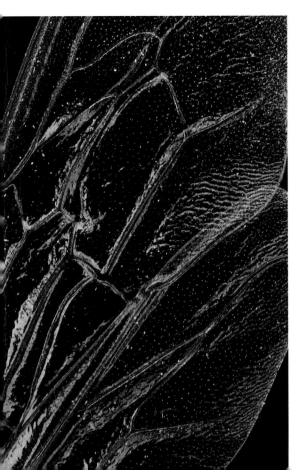

Growing up as a Worker

The queen honeybee lays her egg (above left)
in the bottom of a brood cell. All honeybees
start as an egg. Though only one egg is laid at
a time in a brood cell, there may be up to
30,000 brood cells in a healthy colony.

The egg hatches into a *larva*. At first the
larva eats a rich food called *royal jelly*. But
after three days, the workers and drones are
given much less royal jelly. Instead they are
fed mostly pollen and honey. Only the larvae
which are going to be queens are fed royal jelly
during the whole larval stage. The larva is a
legless white grub (above right) that does
nothing but eat and grow.

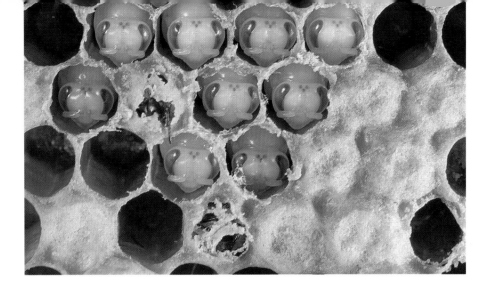

After about five or six days, the larva becomes a *pupa* (above). The body of the larva breaks down and rearranges into the body of an adult honeybee. Its skin darkens and hardens within its brood cell, and after eight to nine days it emerges as an adult.

The new worker honeybee at the center of this photo is just emerging from its waxy brood cell, helped by an older worker.

The Importance of the Queen

The queen (marked in this picture with yellow paint) spends much of her time moving around the brood comb, laying eggs. She is always attended by nearby workers, which constantly touch her with their antennae, picking up her *queen substance.*

The queen substance is a very important pheromone. With this chemical, the queen controls the lives and behavior of the worker bees. As the substance is passed from bee to bee, its scent prevents their ovaries from developing, and it stops them from building queen cells and rearing new young queens.

As the queen honeybee ages, she produces less queen substance and fewer eggs. If there is not enough substance to reach all of the workers, they begin to build queen cells in preparation for the reigning queen's death. The queen cells hang down from the normal comb. An existing larva is fed only royal jelly and emerges as a new queen. When the queen dies, up to 20 queen cells are built.

The loss of queen substance also means many workers' ovaries will develop. They will lay unfertilized eggs, which develop into drones. If no queen is produced, the colony will die out.

Working in the Nest

When a honeybee is young, it works on different tasks in the nest. As it gets older, it works outside. These workers are putting wax caps on cells filled with honey.

At first, workers clean out empty cells for future use. They also fix wax caps on food cells (right) and brood cells. To build up her wax glands, the worker eats lots of pollen and honey. As she ages, special glands in her head produce royal jelly, which she will feed to the young larvae.

The worker honeybee receives nectar from forage workers (above). She airs the nectar in her mouth, ripening it into honey. After it has begun to thicken, she places the nectar into a cell, where it will continue to ripen. The worker bee then can produce enough wax to build additions to the comb. She may also begin feeding the queen larvae. The same worker will then begin to pass nectar back to other workers. Soon, her term as a hive bee will end.

Out in the Meadow

When a worker bee begins her work outside the nest, she will already have made orientation flights into the meadow.

Her first task as an outside worker, if the air is hot, is to ventilate the nest. Hundreds of worker bees stand just outside the nest (above) and fan their wings, cooling the nest to the correct temperature of 95°F (35°C). Another task before she begins her work as a forager is guarding the nest (right). Bees can recognize their nest mates by scent and will attack unfamiliar bees and other intruders.

When a worker bee attacks and stings an enemy, she will give off an alarm pheromone from a gland near her stinger. This alerts other workers to the danger, and they join in the stinging. The defending guards may also bite the enemy with their jaws, giving off a different scent from a gland in their heads.

Some workers will never become guards, but eventually all workers become foragers, searching for food in the flowers of the meadow (above).

Dancing in the Dark

When a worker bee has discovered a good source of nectar and pollen, she returns to the colony to communicate her good news to other members. The worker performs a special dance that shows the distance of the flowers. When they are nearby, the bee runs in a series of circles — called the round dance — and deposits nectar she has brought from the source. Attentive workers lap up the nectar and memorize its scent. Then, they leave the nest in search of the source.

When the food source is far away from the nest, the worker performs a slightly different dance, called the waggle dance. She must now tell the direction of the flowers, as well as the distance. She does this by moving in a course shaped like a figure eight (below).

When she makes the run between the two halves, she waggles her abdomen rapidly. The number of waggles indicates the distance. The direction is shown by the angles of the figure eight. Other worker bees follow her movements carefully, translating the dance into directions, and quickly find the food source.

Drones and Mating

When the weather is good, and the food supply
is ample, honeybees rear drones and mate.
The drone (above) is larger than the workers
and has larger eyes. The queen deposits an
unfertilized egg in special cells built larger for
the drones. When drones hatch, they are very
hungry and eat for about 12 days until they
leave the nest to mate.

The eggs that are to become females are
fertilized with a small amount of *sperm*, which
the queen has stored in her body since she
mated with a drone.

After several orientation flights, the drones gather in a group of many hundreds or even thousands (below). When an unmated queen flies by, they follow behind her in a cluster, following her scent. One drone will mate with the queen in the air and fall to the ground. His penis, which transferred the sperm from his body to hers, remains in her body, and he soon dies. The many drones that do not mate are killed by the workers.

Young Queens and the Colony Cycle

The queen hatches from a special cell built out from the brood comb (above). After hatching, the young queen kills the old queen and the unhatched queens. She mates with several drones and then has enough sperm to fertilize all the eggs she will ever lay. If the colony is overcrowded, or if there is not enough food, the old queen and half the workers and drones leave the hive (below) in a swarm to create a new colony.

↑

The swarm of bees settles on a nearby tree, while scouts seek out a new nesting place. While the bees wait, they live off honey stored in their *crops*. When the scouts discover a good place, they return to the swarm and perform dances similar to the waggle and round dances that show the location of the new nesting place. They will have marked the place with a special scent, so new scouts can find and recognize it.

At the new nest, workers quickly build a new comb and forage for pollen and nectar. The queen is fed and begins to lay eggs, and the colony settles into its routine. Meanwhile, the young queen at the original nest has taken over.

23

Enemies

↑

These Carmine Bee-eaters nest in a riverbank in West Africa. These and other birds eat thousands of bees, especially honeybees. The painful sting of the honeybee is not enough defense against some birds and various other animals. In North America and Europe, woodpeckers drill holes in honeybee hives.

In Japan, 20 to 30 Mandarin Hornet workers can together kill 5,000 to 25,000 honeybees in a few hours. They then take the larvae, pupae, and remaining adults back to their nests to feed to their own larvae.

↑

The Honey Badger, or Ratel (above), lives in Africa and India. It breaks nests open with its powerful claws and eats honey and larvae. The Honey Badger is often led to a nest by a bird called the honey guide. The bird is not strong enough to rip open the nest itself, so it calls attention to the hive and lets the Honey Badger do the work. After the Honey Badger has taken what it wants, the honey guide feeds on what is left of the honeycomb.

This white crab spider can hide easily in the white part of a flower, and it can easily catch and feed on a honeybee.

↓

Friends and Neighbors in the Meadow

The honeybee visits the meadow for food, and it must share the flowers with many other insects and animals that live in the meadow. One of these insects is the Meadow Grasshopper (above). Crickets and grasshoppers match their surroundings so well that their predators have a hard time spotting them.

Some insects use the flowers as places to find each other for mating, or as a place to watch for prey. Other creatures that live in the meadow include centipedes, rabbits, butterflies, mice, and snails (below).

Other kinds of bees may compete with the honeybee for the food of the flowers. The fat, furry bumblebee (above) may help the honeybee in a way. There are both long- and short-tongued species of bumblebees. Short-tongued bumblebees break into comfrey flowers at their base, where the nectar is. Honeybees follow behind and feed through the hole that the bumblebee has made (below).

Honeybees and People

Honeybees have always been valued for their honey and wax. Today, honeycombs and bee grubs are a source of food for people in Africa, especially when there is a food shortage.

At one time, honey was the only sweetener available. People moved wild colonies in logs to protect them. Modern hives (above) have replaced the logs and made it possible to harvest honey and wax, but we have never actually tamed the bees themselves.

In North America, beekeepers travel with their bees, pollinating farmers' crops as they go. The farmers benefit from having their fruit trees pollinated by bees, and the beekeepers benefit from the honey created from the blossoms. Honeycomb wax is used to make fragrant candles and lipstick and other cosmetics. The poison of the worker bees is used to make different medicines.

People have long been fascinated by honeybees and by the orderly structure of their beehive. On the left is a bronze bee from the Gallo Roman period. On the right is an illustration from a 15th-century book about plants.

Life in the Meadow

The honeybee is part of a complex network of survival in the meadow. Plants and animals depend on each other for food. Insects get their food from plants and are eaten by other animals. Those animals are then eaten by larger animals. So food and energy pass from the plants to the honeybee to the other animals through what we call a food chain.

Food Chain

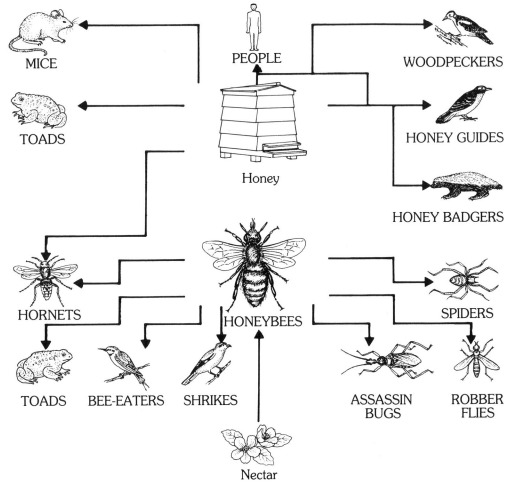

MICE

PEOPLE

WOODPECKERS

TOADS

Honey

HONEY GUIDES

HONEY BADGERS

HORNETS

HONEYBEES

SPIDERS

TOADS   BEE-EATERS   SHRIKES

ASSASSIN BUGS

ROBBER FLIES

Nectar

Grazing animals are important for keeping coarse grasses from crowding out the wild flowers that honeybees depend on. Trees and bushes serve as landmarks to help bees find their nests and sources of food.

Meadows teem with all sorts of life. But unfortunately, meadows are becoming rare. The development of urban areas and farmland has taken over the land that once was home to so many plants and animals.

Wildlife and conservation groups work to encourage farmers and landowners to leave some land for the meadow habitat.

Index and New Words About Honeybees

These new words about honeybees appear in the text on the pages shown after each definition. Each new word first appears in the text in *italics*, just as it appears here.

antennae ...... feelers on the head used for smelling and touching. **7, 12**

caste .... one of several types of individuals living in the colony of a social insect species. **6**

compound eye .... an eye made up of thousands of facets, each with its own lens and nerve connection to the brain. **7**

crop .... a pouchlike sac in which food may be stored or partially digested. **23**

drone .... a male honeybee, which develops from an unfertilized egg. **6, 7, 9, 10, 13, 20-22**

larva (larvae) . the form of an insect which emerges from the egg. **10, 13-15, 24, 25**

ocellus (ocelli) . simple eyes, found in insects, with a single thick lens that can sense changes in the brightness of daylight. **7**

ovaries .... female sex organs in which eggs are produced. **9, 12, 13**

pheromone ... a chemical messenger or scent produced by one animal that affects the behavior of another individual of the same species. **7, 12, 17**

proboscis ...... a tubular structure like a drinking straw through which insects suck up liquid food. **6**

pupa (pupae) . the stage in the growth of an insect when much of the larva is broken down and re-formed into an adult. **11, 24**

queen .... the egg-laying female caste of social insect species. **6, 7, 9, 10, 12, 13, 15, 20-23**

queen substance ..... a pheromone produced by glands in the head of a queen honeybee that prevents workers from rearing other queens and laying eggs. **12, 13**

royal jelly ..... a special food made in the heads of worker honeybees that is fed to honeybee larvae. **10, 13, 14**

segment .... one of several parts forming the body or parts of the body of an insect. **7, 9**

sperm .... (short for *spermatozoa*) male sex cells that fertilize the eggs of the female. **20, 21, 22**

thorax .... the middle of the three body parts of an insect, containing the flight muscles and bearing the wings and six legs. **5, 8**

Reading level analysis: SPACHE 3.5, FRY 3.5, FLESCH 89 (easy), FOG 4, SMOG 3
Library of Congress Cataloging-in-Publication Data
Harrison, Virginia, 1966-
        The world of honeybees / text by Virginia Harrison; photographs by Oxford Scientific Films.
            p. cm. -- (Where animals live)
        Rev. ed. of: The honeybee in the meadow / text by Christopher O'Toole.
        Includes index.
        Summary: Describes the appearance, life cycle, social order, and activities of honeybees that live in the meadow.
        ISBN 0-8368-0142-3
        1. Honeybee--Juvenile literature. 2. Meadow fauna--Juvenile literature. [1. Honeybee. 2. Bees.] I. O'Toole, Christopher. Honeybee in the
meadow. II. Oxford Scientific Films. III. Title. IV. Series.
        QL568.A6H34   1989   595.79'9--dc20   89-33936

**North American edition first published in 1990 by Gareth Stevens Children's Books, RiverCenter Building, Suite 201, 1555 North
RiverCenter Drive, Milwaukee, WI 53212, USA**
US edition, this format, copyright © 1989 by Belitha Press Ltd. Text copyright © 1990 by Gareth Stevens, Inc.
First conceived, designed, and produced by Belitha Press Ltd., London, as **The Honeybee in the Meadow**, with an original text copyright by Oxford
Scientific Films. Format copyright by Belitha Press Ltd. Series Editors: Mark J. Sachner and Carol Watson. Art Director: Treld Bicknell. Design:
Naomi Games. Cover Design: Gary Moseley. Line Drawings: Lorna Turpin.

The author and publishers wish to thank the following for permission to reproduce copyright material: **Oxford Scientific Films Ltd.** for pp. 6 both,
7, 8, 10 both, 11 both, 12, 13, 14, 15 both, 16, 17 below, 18, 20, and 22 above (David Thompson); title page, pp. 3, 4 below, 5 above, 28, 31, and
back cover (G. A. Maclean); pp. 17 above, 22 below, 23, and 27 below (G. I. Bernard); pp. 4 above and 26 above (Mike Birkhead); p. 2 (Stan
Osolinski); p. 5 below (Alastair Shay); p. 9 left (J. A. L. Cooke); p. 21 (Georgina Dew); p. 24 (Michael Fogden); p. 25 below (Derek Bromhall); p. 26
below and front cover (Martin F. Chillmaid); p. 27 above (John Cheverton); Carolina Biological Supply Company for p. 9 right; Partridge Productions
Ltd. for p. 25 above (Anthony Bannister) and p. 19; Photographie Giraudon, Paris, for p. 29 both.

Printed in the United States of America
1 2 3 4 5 6 7 8 9 96 95 94 93 92 91 90
For a free color catalog describing Gareth Stevens' list of high-quality children's books, call 1-800-341-3569.